Master

Consultant

Real Advice
To Take Your Career
To the Next Level

Jason Bear

Copyright © 2020 Jason Bear
All rights reserved.
ISBN: 979-8-6455-3772-2

Contents

Introduction 1

What is a Master Consultant? 3

Chapter 1: The Foundational Skills 5

    Communication Skills..5

    Presentation Skills..6

    Practice..7

    Preparation 8

Learn Presentation Techniques and Technology 9

    Embrace Multitasking..10

    Technical Skills..11

    Time Management 11

Journal Entry: How Urgent is this really?........13

Chapter 2: Develop Your Superpowers 15

    How to Negotiate 15

    How to Deal with Conflicts and Difficult Customers 16

    Take Breaks, Mini Vacations...........................18

    Focus on Your Strength and Learn How to Find Resources...19

    Learn How to Interview 21

Journal Entry: Be Proactive, Not Reactive 23

Chapter 3: Your Mindset 26

- Self-Improvement 26
- Reading Books 27
- Learning from Others 27
- Avoid Procrastination 28
- Become Trustworthy 29
- Work Smart 30
- Create Your Brand 30
- Goal Setting 31
- Always Be the Student, Keep Learning 32

Journal Entry: You're on Your Own 33

Chapter 4: Reading Your Client 36
- Listen and Understand 36
- Resistance 38
- Hesitation 39
- Controlling 40
- Hand Holding 41
- Get Your Team Involved 42

Chapter 5: Complicated Customer Situations .. 44
- Overpromising from Sales 44
- Customer Escalations 45
- You Know of the Issue, but the Customer Does Not 46
- You Don't Know the Answer 47

Journal Entry: People Leave Managers, Not Companies..48

Chapter 6: Career Paths..................................51
- You're the Big Fish......................................52
- You're a Small Fish.....................................53
- Moving Up by Moving Out..........................59
- You're the Boss..60

Journal Entry: Bend the Rules..........................61

Chapter 7: Be in the Top 1%..........................63
- Learn Psychology..63
- Appearances Matter....................................64
- Cut Your Losses Early.................................65
- The Power of Saying No.............................65
- Try Delegating..66
- Stay One Step Ahead..................................67
- Master Your Emotions, Stay Professional....68
- Be Likeable..69

Chapter 8: Know When to Get Out................70
- Physical Health...71
- Mental Health...73
- Your Drive..73

Chapter 9: Outlook for Professional Service Consulting..75

Introduction

When a company purchases a product or service to help better their business operations, it's the role of the professional service consultant to advise and help implement the solution to maximize its benefits while adhering to the fundamental requirements.

The career of a professional service consultant revolves around understanding the scope and limitations of both the service offerings and the business as it operates today.

As a matter of fact, businesses understand the importance of consultants. Back in 1997, US businesses spent $12 billion on consulting, and this was more than 20 years ago. The world has surely evolved a lot during this period, and the role of a consultant has only become critical.

In simple words, the role of a consultant is to consult. Nothing else. What separates a good consultant from a great consultant is the drive and passion for excellence. This book is meant to help give you real business world advice to pinpoint areas where you can improve and give you out of the box thinking strategies as a Master Consultant would do.

Before you commit your career as a professional service consultant, here is what you must know:

- Rewarding pay, but long working hours

And this only intensifies as you become a Master Consultant.

What is a Master Consultant?

A Master Consultant is knowing you are one of the top advisors and trusted professional by your customer and peers. There is no way this can be measured by statistics, records or analytics. But there is a sense of how good you are over others in the same field.

You have the quality of work that is consistent and a confidence that is unwary to face any on the job situations. You understand you are here to first and foremost serve your customers.

The steps in becoming a Master Consultant is something that you do for you. You're taking the time to invest in yourself.

Here are some common traits and situations that a Master Consultant will be familiar with:
- *Management says they need you on this account to help save it*
- *You peers come to you frequently for advice and help*
- *Customers seem to warm up to you easily and have honest conversations*
- *Team members breathe a sigh of relief when they know you have joined the project team*
- *You are always asking many questions and provide 1 or 2 solutions*

- *You take a difficult conversation with the customer as a welcoming challenge*
- *You feel it rewarding mentoring other team members*
- *You are not worried that your job is at risk as you always have the confidence in your skills*

Chapter 1: The Foundational Skills

Being a professional service consultant can be an exciting and high-energy career that keeps you motivated and passionate about the work you do. It requires you to have people skills and the ability to multitask which do not develop overnight.

You have got to work for it and build a solid foundation of strategic competence and skills required to land and sustain a promising career as a professional service consultant.

No amount of enthusiasm and readiness for a career can make up for the lack of fundamentals required. You need to make sure your basics are proficient.

So, here are the fundamentals that you need to be strong at if you are looking at a future in professional service consultancy.

Communication Skills

Any service-based task rests on the basic skill of people management. Communication forms the heart line of anything involving people. As a professional service consultant, you will be interacting with a lot of people.

Your clients, your employers, your peers, the different teams in your organizations and third party vendors will usually use the service consultant as the point of contact for any task.

This means that being able to understand the intended message and delivering the information in the best possible way is a key skill you should master.

This demands that you have sufficient knowledge of the languages used, the modes of communication used and the basics of social etiquette to make a good impression on every communication you make.

You need to understand the underlying psychology to be able to deliver messages at the proper time.

Communication skill is a learned one. Start with brushing some of the skills listed below:
- Listening skills
- Language and vocabulary
- Email writing
- Empathy and patience
- Train yourself in technical jargon and lingo used in your field of work.
- Be calm and professional in all modes of communication.

Presentation Skills

While presentation skills can be considered as an extension of communication skills, as a professional consultant, it mostly involves public speaking which can demand an improved finesse on vocabulary and confidence. These skills cover areas like your ability to frame information in a presentable manner, your body language, tone of your voice and more. The key here is to know your audience. Are you presenting in a stakeholder meeting? Then talk their language and know what they want, just the facts. If you're presenting to technical resources, change you're tone and get more into the details.

This does not change much when you're presenting virtual. In fact, the key here is to make sure the participant maintain engagement. Pause often, use the chats and poll features that comes with the service if it's a meeting longer than 30 minutes. On the flip side you're probably multitasking, so you get it.

Disseminate information in an engaging and informative manner. Here are some ways you can improve your presentation skills.

Practice

The more you practice, the more confident you will be in delivering your presentation. Talk about something you're passionate about that comes out naturally. It could be your work, or it could be a hobby. You don't want to be reading off a script or even trying to memorize what you've written down. That takes away from the natural messaging you'll be in when presenting in the workplace. Practicing by talking to a mirror will not work. You have to video record yourself. Watch it and dissect yourself. Remember, what is a master consultant? While watching yourself on video, is that what you see? If not, keep working on it.

You'll often find some quirks about yourself you didn't even realize you had. This helps to brush up your overall communication and appearance. Here's a tip I've used: to help maintain eye contact look at the middle where the eyes meet just below the gap of the eyebrows. The person you're looking at will not notice.

Preparation

Be completely aware of the topic and the information you are presenting. It could be a process improvement discussion or that subject matter expert that was brought in to add value to the conversation. Whatever the case is, you need to be truly knowledgeable of what you are presenting. If not, does not matter how much you practice you'll look stupid. Mike Tyson said it so precisely "Everyone has a plan until they get punched in the face". There will be people in the group who wants to show their knowledge off and will interrupt you if they hear something that doesn't make sense.

I'm not saying you must know everything and answer all the questions immediate. However, you must be able to play the part well to invoke confidence in your position. Have a couple of repertoires to help recover from times where you don't know how to respond. I call these for a lack of a better term, stalling tactics. For example, in a situation you're being specifically asked about the legislation rule and you vaguely remember the answer, get up, go to the white board or setup an easel with paper, looking for a marker then asking the person again "can you repeat?" You're writing it down. This alone will give you a minimum of 3 minutes to think of a way to respond to the question while still looking like you're taking an importance to point being made.

Learn Presentation Techniques and Technology

PowerPoint is the standard. Make sure you have a good working knowledge of slides structuring and infographics to be presented through a PPT. You can also take advantage of any novel methods that will help make a good presentation. Prepare your slides, printouts, models, and materials beforehand and make sure they are flawless.

If presenting through a web conference, make sure you know how to work with such systems. Get setup earlier than everyone else. Make yourself familiarized with the environment you will be presenting.

The little things like making sure you know how to control the remote. Trying to figure it out while the meeting is underway might put a dent into your natural flow.

Use your practice and preparation to build confidence and develop a positive attitude while presenting. The more comfortable you feel with yourself; you'll start to see the customer feel more comfortable as well.

Embrace Multitasking

Just as mentioned above, using a stalling tactic is the simplest example of multitasking. It's so simple, yet so impactful. Try giving yourself an advantage. Whether it's thinking ahead of the next question or being able to complete two tasks while attending a virtual meeting, multitasking is one of the most impactful skills that a professional service consultant can use.

You should be willing to take up demanding tasks, grasp the underlying requirement and work with multiple teams, clients and peers to get it done on time. This requires you to be flexible to take up multiple roles in a project as per the need.

You can develop your multitasking skills with the help of the right mindset. Here are some tips

- Make an action plan of the activities required to be done
- Learn to prioritize and focus
- Work on similar tasks
- Learn to delegate the simple stuff
- Take proper breaks to review your activities and always plan ahead

Technical Skills

While a professional service consultant is expected to fill in different varieties of tasks, they are also expected to be experts in the particular field of business they are hired to work for.

For instance, if you work as a consultant in the marketing business, you will have to learn the technicalities around it. You should be able to analyze existing strategies, current scenarios and be able to work with the marketing team to make better strategic decisions.

Similarly, your services might be in demand for a variety of business needs like technology, financial planning, and legal advice. You should be able to demonstrate your technical knowledge of the concerned scope of the job.

If the firm you're doing work for has a specific software or application, they are selling, it's not rocket science, but you must master it. Trainings are not enough. You need exposure in real life situations and how the technology works in the real world for customers. In the early stages, ask to be put on projects, make yourself available, tag along a solid consultant whose knowledge of the product you can leverage. This will take some time, even a couple years, so keep at it.

Time Management

All I'm going to say about this is obvious. If you don't have time management, you will not succeed. Make yourself familiar with planning tools and time-saving technologies to effectively manage your time. Outlook is my saving grace.

Journal Entry: How Urgent is this really?

"I know when you're bluffing. I'm a master myself"

When you have a difficult customer, it adds extra demands to your everyday communications. A superb strategy is to constantly question them. This type of customer is always on the offensive and looking to bully their way to through the project. They are not expecting to be running back on defense so stealing the ball is a great way to get them on their tippy toes.

Customer: "This has been a request from the start and now it's not acceptable to hear it's not going to be ready soon. We need to have this report developed by End of Day tomorrow!"

Master Consultant: "What the driving factor to have this completed by tomorrow?"

The customer will think about it and make up something that their team is only available tomorrow or some crucial person to the project must have it.

Master Consultant: "Knowing that this request is probably not going to be completed by tomorrow, can I personally contact this person to understand the information they need?"

The customer might come back saying something else about reiterating the escalation, but you must let them respond don't matter how awkward it gets, don't say a word until they do. Silence is golden.

Listen to what they say and challenge them again. You're not trying to get out of the situation, because at the end the customer paid for it and you want to be on their side.
Sometimes it's the customers fault for not providing the requirements when you asked or needed it. Sometimes it's your team's inability to deliver but it's always ok to challenge the customer, especially when they are a difficult bunch. They must understand that you'll always support your team, but also get them what they need.
They will respect you at the end of the day and will come prepared the next time.

Chapter 2: Develop Your Superpowers

Professional service consultants are supposed to help their clients implement a variety of short term and long-term business needs. This means that businesses are looking for highly competent employees who can adjust to the fast-paced nature of a consultant's job. You need to make a visible impression and be able to get things done. This calls for some specific super skills that go beyond basic communication skills. These skills, if developed, will skyrocket your career allowing you have the ability to demonstrate them.

How to Negotiate

A professional consultant acts as the face of the company to a client. When you make a recommendation, make it difficult for the customer to go against what you said. This requires a good amount of negotiation skills. And worry not as with any skill, you can develop your negotiation skills when you get to know the basics of psychology and the particular need of the person you are negotiating with. It is after all, in essence, an advanced communication skill.

Here are some points to help you be a better negotiator:
- Do not shy away from your objective. Be confident to start the conversation and try to steer it in a positive direction.

- Be knowledgeable about the topic and prepare for different scenarios and options to be presented during negotiation. Plan for the worst outcome while working towards the best.
- Make tradeoffs that make sense to you. This again requires you to have done extensive research.
- Be patient and always conduct yourself professionally
- Never agree to something you're not comfortable with
- It's ok to leave a negotiation without a conclusion

Both sides must feel like they have won something. The customer must feel like they are getting true value. You must feel like you'll gain valuable knowledge or feel financially rewarded.

How to Deal with Conflicts and Difficult Customers

One thing you should always remember as a professional service consultant is to never take anything personal. You are doing your job and that means you will have to face difficult customers at some point. In fact, it could be your specialty. You should be clear-headed and be patient to tackle any challenging situation. One point that always makes it easier for me is to understand it's not you. You're just put into this position. It could have been someone else right now. It just so happens it's you. Don't take it personal. "It's the position you're in, it's not you".

You can have a plan and read as many books as possible but until you're in a sticky situation you really won't know how to act. Everyone is different. Your tolerance level, the way you react to stressful situation will not be the same as others who advise you what to do. My advice is to just experience it and see how you naturally react. I got to a point where I would welcome challenging situations. I would sometimes smile on the inside when I hear the wheels turning and seeing the customer start to get angry. I knew this was going to be a growing opportunity and add to my knowledge base. Gaining knowledge has a lot more to do with being exposed to a variety of situations. So, make sure to always do a post-mortem when you go through a difficult situation with a customer and critique yourself on what you could have done differently to get a better outcome. Nevertheless, here are some key notes that has helped me. Take away what may work with you.

- Be neutral most of the time, not all the time.
- Be aware of your tone, remain empathetic but unaffected. Be nice but don't give in.
- Be patient when dealing with difficult customers. Give time and listen, but make sure you also give them a limit and then respond.

- Try to understand the underlying cause of the situation. Ask open ended questions to get a customer to let it out. This helps ease the conversations without providing a solution.
- Understand your role. If you're playing the subject matter expert in one area and it's a financial issue the customer is having, don't even bother with it. Show your understanding and send the message to the "higher ups".
- If you're able to do so, cut the cord if the situation is out of hand. If you're not, ask to be removed from the project if it's really a crazy situation.

Later in this book, I've highlighted common situations and how to go about them with the customer. If you choose to look now. It's the chapter on: **"Complicated Customer Situations"**

Take Breaks, Mini Vacations

The career of a professional consultant can be both financially rewarding and very exhausting. Constant interfacing with clients and honing your skills can be stressful.

So, remember to take breaks now and then and refresh your mind and body. It's necessary for a master consultant. You must be at the optimal condition to carry out your demanding duties.

You may have to travel a lot as part of your job, and this can be quite exhausting and stressful. Traveling makes you tired and put a strain on your personal life. It takes it to another level because you're not physically present with your loved ones. I personally was in this loop, I would get home on Friday night, Saturday was only available day and Sunday I would fly out again. This was for about 6 months straight. Some weeks I was just too exhausted, I would stay on location like saying to myself "it's just one day is worth it?" What I end up doing from the advice of a mentor is clearing my calendars on Friday. I would reject any meeting requests this day. Friday was my day to catch-up if I wanted to. It was an open day for me.

Make sure you have the necessary means to unwind, so you can start the next day on a positive note. A good state of mind is very crucial for a master consultant as it directly reflects on your craft. Make a conscious effort avoid burn out. Take up effective time management to have proper leisure time.

Focus on Your Strength and Learn How to Find Resources

Everyone is different. Understand your own needs, strengths, and weaknesses. You stand out by the strengths that come easier to you. However, your body of work depends on how you deal with the weaknesses. If you work for a good structured organization, they help you focus on a specific segment, industry or subject, while having others focus on different areas than you. Your weaknesses are not totally exposed, and you can have a good career as a consultant.

That's why I suggest trying to move around early in your career to get much as possible exposure. See what you're drawn too. This is knowing what type of consultant you are and can be. For example, do you like the technical conversations? Are you more inclined to problem solve? Maybe you like being in the forefront of meetings. This shapes your career and give you what you should focus on. You have your angle. I'm so and so and I'm the best at discussion your data transformation challenges. Or let's put her on this project, she knows so much about the legislation and makeup of the banking sector.

Now that you know your strength(s), what's something you struggle with? That's where your team comes in. Sometimes you're thrown to the wolves, if you work for that kind of company, this is where your network of professionals is needed. It could just be simple as let me chat with the "IT" guy he might know something. Be open and helpful to others. If someone reaches out to you, it's because you know your stuff. When you're in that position to seek help, build your "team". On teams (formerly Skype for business), I create my own named groups and contacts within them anytime I need some information. I even have contacts in my phone that their last name is set as "US Taxes". The hard part is finding these contacts. As you build your experience with different projects and firms always reach out to others and build relationships. Look for mentors and those you know are strong subject matter experts. Seek out master consultants. Stay engaged with them and if the opportunity presents itself, attend social outings. Build your network.

Being a jack of all trades is a master of none. Be well versed enough in your industry to be able to at least have a conversation about each topic. But focus your learning and practice on the skills you like and are good at.

Remember, you are looking for help from other subject matter experts. You are not looking for someone to run a meeting for you, craft your emails, talk to clients on your behalf etc.... A master consultant will handle their communications in addition to the tasks he/she is responsible for.

Learn How to Interview

Learning to interview will make you a good listener. It helps you analyze the actual need behind a demand made by the client. Try to frame questions in different matters to get a clear answer to the actual client expectations. Do not assume anything. Think like a lawyer and ask as many questions as you need to get a clear picture of

requirements and feedback. If you're not fully understanding what is being communicated by the client, you're not doing your job. Just because everyone else in the meeting seems to act like they know, be a leader and clarify. Trust that you are one of the smartest persons in the meeting and if you don't know what they're talking about, those other people probably don't know either. They're just scared to raise a hand. Learn techniques on how to ask the same question in different ways.
- What do you mean by that?
- Can you give me an example?
- Can you show me what you mean?
- If we did X, Y and Z, does that solve your problem? What else is missing?

Get the answer you need to move forward.

Journal Entry: Be Proactive, Not Reactive

"If you're proactive, you focus on preparing. If you're reactive, you end up focusing on repairing." - John C. Maxwell

When someone's pressuring you to make a decision you're not sure about, simply buy time and say: "I'll think about it." This phrase can instantly lift the psychological pressure and put you in greater control of the situation. Whether it's an acquaintance asking for a favor or a straightforward ask, take the time you need to evaluate the pros and cons of the situation.

I've taken the approach to think like a road map. To always be a step ahead you must not just provide a response but anticipate how the customer will react and what additional responses you can have. It's not always right however, it gets you in the mindset of thinking ahead. This practice is used by the best businesspeople in all industries to assess how they can react to future forecasts. Trust me this has been very beneficial in my career and seeing where I want to steer my career personally in addition to project situations you will encounter.

Majority of the time, we knew a customer's requirements could not be fulfilled by our standard offering alone. So, in finalizing the requirements we don't just say this "can't be done", we do a deep dive into the requirements, asked various questions as to why they needed it. Basically, make sure this is a real and hard requirement by the person asking for it. If it seems so, let's involve more of the customer's team and asked the same questions in follow-up meetings gauging how important this requirement really is. In my example, we had a few members of their team questioning as to why they were internally doing it this way and what were they trying to solve. Realizing they were not trying to solve a business issue, but an issue with the process that one person was used to doing in order to help them reconcile their numbers, we were able to provide a positive consultative solution that brought a process change to the business. The person who brought up the requirement as a showstopper did feel negativity towards me because of in a way exposing their work on a microscope for their colleagues to see. I've learnt this is expected, you won't win over everyone, however, you need to think of the bigger picture and what is right for both the business you serve for and the customer experience. This could have ended up in us providing a "work around" solution for this one person that would have worked only for this person. If that person were to leave, it would be useless. The extra effort on our side to be proactive was worth it.

    Proving results is keeping the power on your side. To stay proactive, document everything, in all meeting notes ensure there is a section for action items. In there put due dates, what must be done and who is leading the charge.

Chapter 3: Your Mindset

As mentioned, one of the essential traits of a master consultant is your confidence. In some ways coined as the consultant mindset. Having the right mindset is what prepares you to be the best consultant that clients and employers can trust. It reflects on your sincerity and the efficiency of every task you undertake.

With your mindset tuned to align with the project demands, you will be able to face most challenges in a highly competitive career like that of service consultancy throws at you. You will have to satisfy different conditions that might seem impossible at first. You will have to weigh in different options, make some hard decisions that are favorable to all parties involved. Having to juggle a lot of considerations can be overwhelming but that is all part of a consultant's job description.

So here are some ways you can develop and sustain that mindset:

Self-Improvement

Never stay complacent. Keep working on improving yourself on what you feel you need is important to get your job done efficiently.

For instance, if there is an opportunity to deal with a high-profile Japanese client, maybe you should start learning basic Japanese etiquette and the language. It could help you communicate better and understand the client's needs easily.

This can be a simple as listening to a couple of pod casts a week.

Reading Books

Make reading books an active hobby. As it is said, reading is to the mind what exercise is to the body. Reading good books is not just entertainment. It is a good way to amass knowledge and improve your communication skills.

When you are trying to learn more about something, the internet is a great resource, but I find getting your head in an actual book is just so much more accurate and real.

Reading helps you with concentration and acts as a mindful practice to organize your thoughts and boost creativity.

And sometimes books are the best source of information for self-improvement. When you read about successful people elaborating on their journey to success, you will gain the much-needed inspiration and guidance towards self-improvement.

Learning from Others

Do not underestimate the value of human relationships, interactions, and behavior. By observing the people around you, you will get a wealth of information on how you can better yourself. Just because someone is doing better than you, it's not a reason to hate them. Don't compare yourself. Get that shit out your head. We all learn at different paces and some people just have had more help earlier than you.

You can observe your successful friend, notice what they do differently that has helped them reach success. Ask them if it's not obvious. Most successful people are willing to share the wealth of knowledge. In the same way, instances of setbacks can also teach you valuable lessons.

It is considered best to make a learning relationship with basically three types of people.
- Your mentor figure who is in a level where you want to be
- A peer who is on the same level as you are
- Someone whom you can be a mentor to. Someone junior to your level.

This way you can learn how your seniors reached their success, how your peers are working to achieve the same and how the methods are changing with newer generations. This will help you keep updated and motivate you towards self-improvement.

Avoid Procrastination

Whatever you decide to work on and improve, start now. Do not procrastinate. It slows down your momentum and makes you hurry up your tasks at the last minute. I have an extremely difficult time with this one. For me at least, motivation comes in spurts. I could have days where I just can't wait to continue working on a problem and then weeks where I can take the easy road. Thus, knowing how I operate, when I get these days of enthusiasm, I maximize it to the fullest because I know it's a small window I have. Pushing through those lazy cycles is hard but here are some ways you can fight the procrastination monster:

- Schedule your tasks and see that your time is managed properly.
- Take appropriate breaks. If you work for 25 minutes, give yourself a break of 5 minutes.
- Figure out if you're a morning or late-night person and maximize that time for work if possible.
- Work hard during the week knowing that your Friday is a day to take it easy.

Become Trustworthy

An invaluable asset you can develop is the amount of trust you get from your clients and peers. Trust is what makes people open up and lets you help them find better solutions. It is the key to successful communication.

To gain such a good level of trust, It's up to you.

If you promise yourself, you will get better with accounting software, you better put in the effort needed to master it. Be accountable and show your sincerity for self-improvement. Show that you can trust in yourself before you can do it for someone else. Ask yourself, would you rather have you on this project or is someone else better? Tough question but necessary for you to wake up.

Work Smart

Just because you worked 80 hours this week, it's not going to guarantee you results. It's not the number of hours that count but the number of productive hours that count towards betterment. And if you really think the company is making you work so many hours then my friend, you're in the wrong place. You're training yourself to allow work to take priority. Remember, being a master consultant requires a lot of prep work and focus but also allowing yourself time to do turn off and rejuvenate.

Try to be smart about everything you do. Is there is a better way to do something? Has someone else worked on a similar project and you can use the same files as templates to save you the extra work to start from scratch? A steady minded pace is how you work smart.

Create Your Brand

Know your value and learn to market it well. Do not try to be too humble and let up opportunities pass that can make you grow your brand. I'm not a professional at self-promotion, so I'm going to refer you to read the book called "Bad Ass Your Brand" by Pia Silva.

Goal Setting

We have already discussed how setting goals makes you more accountable and time efficient. But the way you set goals determines the way you put your efforts and how it benefits you.

Be smart about your goals. Have long term goals and break them into achievable short-term goals of increasing complexity that will lead you to your long-term goal. Start small, feel a sense of accomplishment early and build your momentum to conquer bigger ones.

I use the world-renowned formula:
- **S**pecific
- **M**easurable
- **A**ttainable
- **R**elevant
- **T**ime oriented

Example: *I will attend a local toastmaster's event to get me started on developing my public speaking. Due Date Aug 15, 2020*

Your goals must be specific, so you should know exactly what you are trying to achieve. These goals are personal, not work related. Set a deadline for your goals so you don't procrastinate forever. And finally, write them down!

Always Be the Student, Keep Learning

It is never too late to learn something new. Keep your brain cells polished and be receptive to any learning opportunity. Stay curious.

This attitude to stay open to learning, helps broaden your scope and perspective. It makes you a reliable person who is ready to listen which is a great quality a good consultant is expected to have.

Constant learning helps you stay relevant in a fast-paced environment and makes you an asset. It makes you flexible and adaptable to any situation which is again an important aspect of a professional service consultant.

Take technology as an example. You must keep up or you'll be the only one still using a flip phone.

Journal Entry: You're on Your Own

"Teach people how to treat you" -
Unknown

Dealing with management that says they support you but doesn't truly know what it means when your back is against the wall.

In this project our client was very demanding. It was probably one of the most draining and time-consuming project's I've ever been a part of and lasted for almost 3 years. I noticed I started new habits that just opened my anxiety box that have been with me even after the project completion. I went through a project manager that quit, an entire overhaul of our implementation consultants just because of exhaustion and fatigue. Also, we changed our sponsor to see if anything would help. This client was just plain difficult and wasn't going to change their ways no matter what we did. Well I take that back. We could have made them change but our management was not willing to implement the changes I proposed. To the clients credit they did it their way and never backed down.

"Teach people how to treat you" is one of my quotes I always seem to reference time and time again and this time it reminds of how impactful it really is.

From the beginning, the client smelt blood and always was on the kill. They felt that our team lacked leadership and used their team to dictate the entire timeline, methodology and hours of work. Yes, you are reading this correctly. They decided when we were to be available. Basically, we were waiting for their call. Doesn't matter the time of day. And most of the time it was after our regular hours because they were in California and most of us being on the east coast. I cannot tell you how upset my team was and so how I was. I know I had the ability to lead us and make better decisions, yet I was powerless in this project.

Title doesn't mean anything if there is no assumed power behind it. So why even have calls, presentation deck and so on... that list our name and title and what was our role? It meant nothing. We struggled, bitched, and a bunch of consultants left the firm just because of this project. We got it done. At the end was it worth it? I mean, the money for the firm? From my side, hell no. We tripled our contracted hours, we gave them customized solutions for free and worst of all we knew at the end of the day we would not even get a happy customer. Management's advice? Push through it!

Looking back, I've learnt a lot from this experience. The customer felt we had no support; we would bend over backwards just to kiss their ass and they took full advantage of it. Good for them. Management in the same breath did the same. Took advantage of their power by having no backbone. It caused our project team, which was a really great team in other circumstances, not only stress to the max but made those few consultants who would of had good careers, change their minds about the profession.

You'll always get those tough customers and for the most part it's a welcoming challenge. But as soon as you see you have no support from your management, you need to communicate straight forward that you want off the project. Do not listen to the sweet talk and have them try to keep you in. Get out, make it clear you don't feel supported. Be brave in your action, don't feel your job is at risk because most of the time they need you more than they need them. If you act quickly and make enough noise, they will reassign you to another project because they know being a master consultant the value you bring to them. Teach people how to treat you.

Chapter 4: Reading Your Client

The best part about being a professional service consultant is the opportunity you get to interact with a wide range of uniquely individuals. People management will be an indispensable part of your career. This calls for some specific skills that let you make the right conversations and steer your client interactions in the best possible direction.

Like we said, they all come from different backgrounds and levels of the corporate ladder and have their own unique needs and behavioral traits. Understanding the nuances of client behavior is necessary to make any type of successful conversation.

This does not have to be a special talent where you must be a genius to figure out whatever the client thinks. All it takes is some careful observations, accumulated experiences, and the right mindset. So, let's see in detail how you can better read your client.

Listen and Understand

The basics of any communication is to listen to what the other person is saying. It does not merely mean hearing whatever they say and waiting for them to finish so you can respond. A lot of people do this, and you'll notice it quickly. Pay careful attention to what the client is trying to say. In other words, what are they asking?

Take a genuine interest in knowing your client. Note down their actual needs and understand their requirements and situation. This will help you dig in deeper and make relevant conversation that will let you get closer to the client. Here is a guideline on how you can start out with reading a client.

- Make an outline of your expectations of a client. And do not assume this is what the client demands. Be well prepared before you meet the client. Try to gather information on the previous dealings with the client or similar projects. Once you've completed the necessary requirements-gathering meetings, compare what they want with what your original expectations were. This will give you an idea of how much effort you will have to really put in based on the differences. If your expectations and understanding of their communicated requirements are similar, you have a prepared client.
- Develop a basic assessment of the client's behavior profile. Try to notice the body language of your client. How they act, the gestures they make, their level of temper, the current mood they are giving off and how comfortable or anxious they are in the moment.
- Be ready to deal with any outlier behavior. For instance, something you say might offend the client or make things go more

personal than they should be. You should have the right mindset and the calm collected behavior to deal with such situations.

Resistance

Certain times you'll be faced with user-based clients who are not willing to participate in the negotiation or will have little interest in investing their time and energy into listening to you. They might be here due to various reasons but that does not mean there is no chance of getting a resistant client to get to your side.

You'll have to intentionally handle the resistance and be able to provide a compelling reason for the client to stay on the right track. Resistance could stem from any underlying cause like contradictory beliefs, conflicts of interest, job security or general lack of interest.

But not all resistant clients are overtly expressive of their contradictions. Some are too polite to express it, and some can be less motivated into contributing to the interaction.

There are certain behavioral cues that let you understand a resistant client. Some common body language like crossing one's arms, feet facing the opposite direction, lack of eye contact, nodding of head without any actual reaction, lack of concentration can all point to a resistant client.

Gestures and body language can be a great way to assess the level of interest a client has in what you offer them. Understand these visual cues and adjust your conversation accordingly to make it more receptive.

Understand the root cause for resistant behavior. Realize their position, their benefit or demise of their role in the goal of the project. For example, they could be implementing a brand new process that in the end reduces their team or even put the person's job at risk when you're all said and done.

Doing so will help you come up with countermeasures to deal with it. In the end, client resistance has no room in contractual projects. Their management decided to move forward with you as their leader of change. In your communications, set deadlines and include additional important stakeholders copied with a resisting individual. If this person doesn't give you the responses you need, you're clear from being the scapegoat as you've documented everything along the way. Make a point to identify these users as a risk. The investment these companies make are more important than one individual you're unable to turn around.

Hesitation

Hesitation is again an emotional blocker to progressing on a project. There might be a reason. For example, the client might usually be someone who needs to take a lot of consideration before finalizing anything. Or sometimes the client may not be sure of themselves or their needs.

A hesitant client might make excuses or feel uncomfortable when you try to push them into a decision. It is important to give the client the space and time they need to make a decision. If you push a hesitant client too much, it might backfire. Then again, if the delays have an impact on the project timeline, get your sponsor involved and point these out as risks on the stakeholder meetings.

Again, body language cues and speech patterns like long pauses and visible discomfort can be indicators of hesitation.

Make sure your client feels comfortable enough. The environment and your attitude should not be intimidating but welcoming to their suggestion. Make sure you give enough validation to their suggestions and serious consideration of their ideas and possible concerns.

Allow them to ask questions freely and make them comfortable enough to clarify all their doubts without condescending responses. That's really the best you can do with a hesitant customer.

Controlling

While you may think customers who are too controlling and customers who are too hesitant to be vastly different, the baseline to their behavior is surprisingly similar. Some clients try to be controlling when they feel they are not understood and are uncomfortable with the way the conversation is going. They try to take back control by cutting in when you talk or outright reject your suggestions.

Dealing with such clients calls for an immense amount of patience and a deeper understanding of how the client views the matter at hand. Try to understand the client's model of view and try to work your pitches that suit their understanding. Be patient and remember not to take any of it as a personal attack. Hold your ground and push back by using the questioning strategy as mentioned in this book.

Words to remember: *it's not who you are, it's the position you are in.*

Hand Holding

There is an underlying cause of the client's behaviors as we discussed. It is the lack of understanding and the need to feel understood without being judged or taken as a slight. It is important that you don't hurt the client's sensibilities trying to be smart.

Their demands, however, ridiculous as it maybe should be dealt with constructive feedback and careful deliberation. Any show of contempt or lack in respect towards the client can lead to an unfavorable situation you both do not want. And that's exactly what a professional service consultant is hired to do.

There should not be a notion of who is right and who is wrong. You must make sure opinions, no matter how contradictory to your standing, should be respected and proper information is delivered to the client.

From time to time you'll get those clients that just need extra help. That's how they learn. You might be contracted to just "hand hold". If so, brace for a long road ahead. Make sure if it's your company, you get compensated well for it. It really does take a lot of time and your time is very valuable. If you have the luxury, delegate this task. This will save you a tremendous amount of time so you can focus on more important tasks.

Get Your Team Involved

No organization runs by one individual effort. Often, it is possible for a dedicated service consultant to take up all the burden and end up getting burnt out or lost in a difficult situation. Especially when it comes to confronting a difficult client.

You have to remember that you work as a team. So, don't shy away from seeking help from your peers and higher ups when the situation asks for it. This makes it easy for you to hand over the responsibility to your teammates, in case of your absence or some unavoidable circumstances.

Another key reason that you must get your team involved is that it builds trust with the client that your team is capable of the tasks ahead. I cannot tell you how many times I've seen clients asking to change members of the project team or just constantly avoid others because that trust is non-existing for the entire team.

Chapter 5: Complicated Customer Situations

As a professional service consultant, complicated customer situation is a common scenario. Just like any relationship, now and then you'll come across disagreements, unfulfilled promises and crazy requirements. How you deal with complicated customer situation is a direct reflection on your personal brand. These are some situations you've most likely faced and some advice on how to better remedy them.

Overpromising from Sales

One of the most difficult situations to start a project is to reset customer expectations. This is part never gets old and with some growing firms sometimes it's a strategy just to get the business. So yes, the account executive said of course we can do this and now it's your job to figure it out. Not always there is a viable solution. In these situations, you must realign expectations immediately. Your responsibility is to provide a path to a solution that you can offer. It might not be your role to communicate it to the customer, but it is your duty to point it out internally so the senior consultant or project leads can deal with it. Step one, put a meeting together with sales to ensure it wasn't a miss communication. Step two, gather internally to brainstorm possible alternative options. Step three, meet with the customer without the sales rep to bring up the issue and the viable options. This doesn't put the salesperson on the hot seat and gives you and the customer to form a common bond. Step four, meet internally after with sales to discuss next steps.

You're in the early stages of your project and even though it's already starting out with a difficult conversation, it's really the best time for it to be happening. It may result in an adjustment in pricing or providing additional services depending on how the customer reacts. Remember the customer has paid for a service so the impact here is financial which is at the end of the day the highest of priority.

Customer Escalations

During the project, you should always be looking out for potential issues. Monitoring known issues and risk is the key to preventing further noise. However, stuff falls through the cracks and if it's important enough, the customer might escalate. Sometimes they go over your head and go straight to the project sponsors and or management. This is not something to worry about for you personally. However, when you become aware of the escalation you must take responsibility of it. This is not a blame game, even though the customer might be pointing the finger at you specifically. Don't get into the game with the customer. They may have dropped the ball, don't point the finer back, but you should always remain calm and provide a path to solution. If it's indeed the customers fault, more often than not, times of weakness shows itself again. There will be ample opportunity later, but like I said don't point the finger back, it's known.

I've learnt to never personally admit to wrongdoing. Instead, generalize it if you're asked to respond. Some good ways to respond are "This is disappointing and I understand the importance of having our attention on the issue", "This is certainly not the first time we've seen this and it won't be the last but it is what it is at this point. Let's move forward on focusing on how we remedy the issue. "

You Know of the Issue, but the Customer Does Not

Why is this even a conversation? You must let the customer know. Being ahead of the customer proves your value to them. You can't control how the customer will react but that doesn't matter. Let them vent if they need. Let them take whatever action they need to on their side. Prior to communicating the issue, make sure you have a path to resolution. What I mean, have at least one way to solve the issue first. Setup the meeting, communicate the issue and discuss the path to resolution. This almost always results in avoiding any escalation as the customer was not ready to react and you've already talked about how we solve it.

You Don't Know the Answer

You're a trusted advisor, so shouldn't you know everything? Not really. You should know a good amount but not everything is black and white. If you're being asked a direct question and you don't know the answer, never guess the correct answer. A good response is "I understand your requirement, but I'm not 100% sure on how we would solution this. Let me take this back until I get more information. I'll follow-up with a meeting" or "Before I confirm my answer, I'd like to review our best practices on this topic before I give you my final answer"

Journal Entry: People Leave Managers, Not Companies

"Don't take the bullshit from an unworthy bigwig"

Once you reach a certain amount of salary, your primary need has less to do with money and more to do with how you are treated and valued.

This manager was getting on my nerve. Taking advantage of his position and being totally ignorant and just straight out rude by lacking common sense on so many levels. I realize in these types of settings; seniority was the only reason he was in that position of a manger. Nothing else. Years of service alone do not translate to skills as a People manager. This is what I found with most large companies. Sometimes you're just a number.

In my case, I just couldn't take how my manager couldn't understand a lot of situations and made me feel dumb for lack of a better term. I knew I had the potential to be something special in this firm and move up the corporate ladder but he was my road black. Your success in a company really does depend a lot on your manager. Remember this. Its best to end this relationship the sooner than later. It can and will impact your professional brand. When I mean end the relationship, if you really like the company, try seeing if you can change teams or departments by going a level higher than your manager. Or leave completely.

In my case, I left. I was working late nights because of special requests from this manager that I knew would not benefit the team or the customer. It was in actuality, helping him with his work. I don't have a general issue with this, but I knew he was using my experience and skills when he was not pulling his weight. Let me tell you the last straw. The deadline was in the morning, a complete project writeup with a charter to be completed by the morning. He was also messaging me late night to also help him do a presentation in PowerPoint. There were more than a few times I know he was using me. So, I spent about 30 minutes after he messaged me that day to write up my letter of resignation. First thing in the morning, I know this nut job would message me to ask about his work. Instead I sent my resignation via email to him, his boss and the firm's partner notifying them I would no longer want to continue effective immediately. There was a good ten minutes of silence until I got a call from the manager above him. He was trying to understand why the sudden change in attitude and was also trying to keep me desperately. I explained the situation fully and ended the call saying my decision is final and that I respected his time to connect with me. Even though he was a nice guy and we had a good relationship, it was too late. It wasn't the first time I brought it up and unfortunately the action is too late. The next call was from my direct manager, the nut job, who a few minutes ago was calling me about his work I had to complete. His tone was fearful and shaken. I realized he must of hand a talk with his manager and partner. He had never been in this position before, like I mentioned he lacked experienced. My answers were short, and I knew he was almost begging me before I left to give him his work but I said I already moved on and that was that. I'm sure he learnt a big lesson.

Don't waste your talents and don't be taken advantage of at the workplace. If you feel you're in this situation, make your move and plan how to address it immediately.

Chapter 6: Career Paths

One of the best things about being a professional service consultant is the steady and continuous growth. It's a skill that allows you to be portable and even independent if you choose.

The career path is one of the most important telltale signs of a successful career trajectory and growth. It forms the basis for further career developments and goals for your future. Each job and role you take up should align with your long-term goals. On average, a person may hold somewhere around 10 to 15 jobs during their entire work career.

Each job is supposed to serve as the ladder through which you climb to achieve success, but it's not always straight forward. Setbacks will happen, promotions will be missed, and you might even get canned. Performing a postmortem after each project is essential to learn about failures, wins and where you could improve. This is the same for your career. After changes, either initiated by you or your employer(s), do the same process. Learn about why you failed, why you had success and where you could have done better. Use it and apply it to your next job. You must keep a journal and write these down just like your goals. Revisit them ever so often.

While the career path for each person may vary and is as unique as the person is, most successful career paths allow for vertical growth. But no matter how you choose to move up, down or even take a break; make sure it aligns with your career values and your expectations. As you know already, job satisfaction is the key to a successful long career.

The outlook for the professional service consultant career is positive because of tech always advancing and businesses looking to improve efficiencies. They need that expert who will understand their needs and implement what they want. Smart businesses will always pay for that type of service. It's up to you to stay up to date with these technologies to keep you serviceable.

You're the Big Fish

Any job role or job switch you make boils down to choices. Do you want to grow upwards to face increasingly difficult challenges and responsibilities or choose to have an unchanging career that doesn't evolve much? The choice is yours. But for a competitive environment like professional service consultancy, it is better to keep moving forward and be ready to embrace new challenges. It's easy to fall out because you need to keep updating your skills.

Be the big fish in any pond you are in. Being in a smaller organization may not offer as much exposure and resources as a bigger organization does. But it gives you better opportunities to grow as a consultant and provides more options for individual learning and growth. Use the opportunities well and you can soon be the big fish at your organization.

Try to get into a small firm, sometimes called boutique firms. I can tell you this is the best way to expand your business knowledge. You're exposed to all departments, operations and to the upper management team. So that's a huge opportunity to learn the consultancy business. Get closer to key people in the organization. Learn how the high performers do their work. Ask to be part of a variety of projects and play different roles, because you can. Expose yourself to much as possible so you build your skills set and decide what areas you like better. You can grow quickly in small firms and turn into the big fish. You know the ceiling and it's up to you if you're ok with that.

You're a Small Fish

A bigger organization has its own perks. They have high status, enforce high standards and exposure to high profile projects and customers. But the hierarchy in big get organizations is more rigid and competition is high – meaning, it will take more time for you to achieve the big fish status. Nevertheless, you must try to aim for the best roles and put in more effort to reach the top for accelerated career growth.

It could take time but remember to set your aims high. Turnover in large firms are very high. If you stick with it long enough, you'll move up. You will not have those opportunities to learn about the business operations and get that variety of exposure, however, opportunity here is still good. The best learning opportunities here are for the soft skills, the standards and process. If you find you lack these skills, it might be a good career change to get into a large firm.

I believe you need a variety of experiences to know what works best for you. Especially, if you have your eyes set out to be your own boss. Don't stay to long in one place or company. Give yourself 2 to 3 years to decide if you want to take the next step in the organization or get out and learn elsewhere.

Craft yourself a career path diagram and fix a timeline on where you see yourself achieving the milestones in your career path.

Here is a generic professional service consultant's career graph:

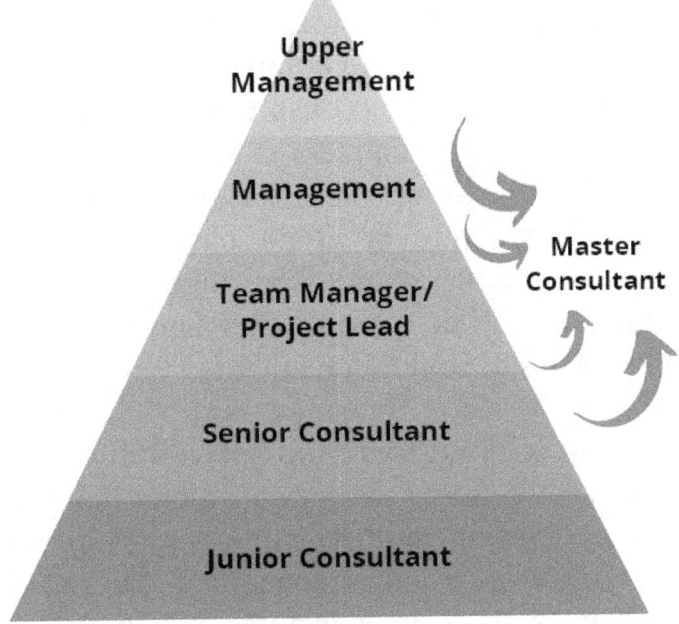

Now, at any level of this growth trajectory, you could choose to move up further to move out to a better position in a different company. The thing to remember is never to settle for a lower position when you move out.

Junior Consultant or Associate

As a beginning into the world of consultancy, you will be placed as a junior / associate consultant in any company. This is how you start your journey as a professional service consultant. So, understand what the job entitles and choose a niche that aligns with your passion and interests. There are several types of consulting businesses and each may have their own consulting methodologies, policies and training programs.

Well-developed huge companies will have clear definitions of your consulting responsibilities, ample work, and resources.

Smaller consulting firms may not have the same ideal infrastructure or client base but will have some interesting work. The hierarchy at these workplaces will be more flexible and you will have direct access to senior consultants.

Trying to go freelance as a junior level consultant will not work. In fact, it will crush your idea of what being a master consultant really is.

Make learning and growth your priority when you start out as a junior consultant. Do not shy to seek help from senior consultants to increase your skill levels. As a junior consultant, you will be given more room for error than you can expect at higher levels. So, give your best at learning the crafts required to become a successful consultant and show your potential to your seniors.

Try to work on different accounts and clients to grow your experience. Remember to follow instructions and try to add value by providing solutions to any existing issues. Be a team player and offer good support to your peers. This is really the best phase of your career.

Senior Consultant

When you move up the ladder to become a senior consultant, you will be expected to take on more serious responsibilities and whatever was nice-to-have when you were a junior will become a must-have. You should be able to put in distinctive individual contributions to the projects that you handle.

You will be working under a supervising manager and may be given additional responsibilities to lead junior consultants. Mistakes will not be tolerated as much, and you will have to put in extra efforts to get recognition and further promotions. This phase will be the hardest and potentially the longest to get out of. This is where you build your brand and can move easily from firm to firm to see where you best fit in. In fact, it's the best opportunity to give freelancing a try to see if you have it. This is where you can become a master consultant.

Manager of a Team / Project Lead

The next step to grow as a service consultant in an organization is, usually, to be a manager of a team and being fully responsible for projects and client accounts.

Team management is a special skill you will have to develop and use efficiently to get the best out of your subordinates. You will be the contact point for both your clients and your team, thereby doubling up your responsibilities. The communications skills, especially the special skills here is where you will shine.

The more you can exhibit your leadership qualities and skills, the easier it will be for you to continue growing in an upward trajectory. Becoming a mentor and giving back starts here. You must make this a part of your responsibilities.

Management / Upper Management

The topmost positions in an organization that take the most important business decisions and shape up the organizational policies and management model form the upper management. They have higher power and highest responsibilities than lower levels of management. Your influence on projects and people are at its maximum.

Your tasks will carry a higher level of importance to the growth of the organization itself and this is the highest you can go in a consulting firm. Becoming a partner or easily transition into owning your own firm. Don't waste your connections here.

Moving Up by Moving Out

The above career path need not always be a straight line in a single organization. More often, you could feel stagnant at a position or circumstances like company take-over and downsizing may mean less growth.

It is okay to move out of a company and look for better opportunities in such cases. While it is good to be loyal to your boss, it doesn't mean you shouldn't give up on your growth aspects. There could be many reasons why you would want a job change.

In terms of career growth, always make sure you have a good amount of experience amassed from your first job to make a switch. If you feel stuck, it is probably time to move. Based on your experience, choose a better role and move to a company where you feel you can move forward.

Give yourself a threshold period which could be anywhere between 1 to 3 years if you don't see your organization valuing your work. Make sure you leave amicably and in a professional manner when you are switching companies. Further, avoid moving down from your position when you are making a switch.

Another great advice to follow would be to use a move out to get a raise. I have learnt this from experience - moving out gives you an opportunity to negotiate your new employment contract based on your experiences and skill levels. The result –

you could end up getting the money you think you deserve.

You're the Boss

When you are confident and have gathered a good amount of experience, you can even look at freelancing options or start up your own consulting firm. Being your own boss has its perks.

You get to decide your working hours and balance your workload efficiently. Many experienced consultants are happy to take up this path given the level of control and rewarding nature of owning your business provides. But it also poses increased risk and responsibility. This is where you know what your made of.

From advice, try starting off part time. Part time will eventually become full time if you're good enough. Jim Rohn said it best "I'm working full time on my job and part time on my fortune"

Journal Entry: Bend the Rules

"Rules are made for the amateurs. Break them only if you have mastered them."

You must do this in a very limited way as you don't want others to know. Customers talk and word spreads fast. So present it in an exclusive way that is almost like hey I know we are not able to do it formally but let me do something special for you guys this time and sympathize with what they are complaining about for the reasoning. Right or wrong you know your limits as a master consultant. Typical examples are building a custom interface, offering more on-site present, or offering custom training that you know something that will be a big help for them. But follow through and deliver your promise as you stated.

Giving them something for free should always be a last resort. Especially since you might have to get approval from higher up or down the road it may need modifications and service teams will need to be aware of what was done. The customer can also use it against you to get more out of you. "Hey, can you do something similar for x,y and z? I don't see how much extra work that would be since you've already created it" Be cautious.

It's true, the noisy wheel gets the oil. You know your customer, use your good judgement on this one.

Chapter 7: Be in the Top 1%

A successful career depends a lot on how favorably you distinguish yourself from the rest of the workforce. And in an environment, such as that of service consultancy, you will be expected to bring in something new for each venture you undertake, and your contribution will have to be indispensable for the company's progress.

Your skill sets and experience should make you a valuable resource that any consultancy would love to hire. Do not settle for mediocrity. Make sure that you stay on the top levels of performance and try to be proactive in all your business interactions.

Aim higher and leave no place for doubts. Keep your focus straight as this is a defining quality of any master consultant.

Here is a rundown of the few ways through which you can achieve and maintain a high success rate in all your client dealings.

Learn Psychology

Well, I don't really mean you have to mandatorily get a degree in psychology to be successful as a service consultant. Having a fundamental understanding of human psychology helps in any career and is even more essential when it is a career that requires you to interface with people.

A big part of a professional service consultant's job is to communicate with different types of people from different spheres of life.

Good knowledge of psychology and observation lets you grasp the subtle body language, mood and intent of the person you are interacting with. Learning who you are talking to and knowing how to talk to them in their setting is a huge asset that will take you to high places as a service consultant.

Appearances Matter

As a master consultant, you will be representing your firm and that means you have to carry a dignified and charming presence that warrants a trustworthy and pleasant environment. The way you carry yourself speaks a lot about your sincerity, confidence and skill levels.

Clients and peers would be instantly willing to deal with you when you look like a champion who looks capable of solving their issues. Pay attention to what you wear and how you present yourself. Be confident. Some of your psychology lessons should help you in this regard as well.

A good rule of thumb is that you must always dress well. First impressions are usually made by the way you dress. If you are unsure how to dress, try to be the best dressed in the room. Don't worry too much being overdressed. Sometimes, it can be a great conversation starter and a good way to get in a laugh or two during your meeting.

If you want to rise to the top and lead the pack, you have got to look the part.

Cut Your Losses Early

Knowing when to back off is one of the most underrated skills people tend to ignore. One unfortunate thing that happens with most promising consultants, even with the ones with a good track record, is that when they face a loss, they tend to overcompensate and aggravate the situations even more.

It is good to be ambitious. But it is better to be wise and ambitious. Remember earlier on, keep a steady pace. Cutting your losses early works the same in professional service consultancy just as it does in financial management. When you know an account is sinking your resources and budget, it's time to evaluate the necessity of supporting it. Learn to make tradeoffs and base your decisions on the facts that you have.

You can also seek help from experts and superiors to come up with proper solutions. If something can't be saved, save whatever else you can. Do not spend your precious time and energy on a project that is not working out as projected.

The Power of Saying No

You should always remember that negotiation is two-way communication. You have as many rights to assert your position albeit professionally and politely as much as the other party does. So, when a proposal or a project so called "opportunity" sounds unfavorable to you, it is completely okay to say No.

Be direct with what terms you can never agree on. There could be many reasons for it such as company policies, loss of value, legalities and more. Don't feel threatened to state negative answers, instead provide the other party with viable options that will let them rethink their position and choose something that works for both of you. This is not just during the project but also at a personal career level with your manager. Make sure people know what you are game for and most importantly, what you're not.

Don't feel bad to say No. It's better than being vague and talking around it in hopes the person on the other end is getting what you're saying. Being straightforward will gain you more trust and will avoid any kind of miscommunication. Remember as a professional service consultant you are expected to be good at people management and not be a people pleaser.

Try Delegating

Delegating work is a must-needed skill that you should possess. Most consultants tend to feel burnt out or are unable to carry out their tasks to perfection because they fail to delegate efficiently. Learn to delegate the right task to the right person.

This is the upper management special skill. Get the right resources to do the job for you. Learn it early on so it makes your life easier and prepare for when you move up.

Trust is an important thing to maintain not just with your clients but also with your team. Learn to trust your team and get others involved to work collaboratively.

Pick the right person for a task and make sure their responsibilities are well defined. Give clear instructions on what you expect to be done and the time frame within which you want the work done. Set realistic expectations and delegate work accordingly. You cannot assign an important task to a newbie who is just learning the fundamentals. Similarly, an experienced person might feel unused if you assign a minor task that is way below their skill set. Make sure you provide the resources needed for them to carry out their tasks and feel valuable.

Finally, always remember to share a few words of feedback, motivation and encouragement to your fellow colleagues to raise morale.

Stay One Step Ahead

Stay ahead. Two words. Easier said than done. It takes a lot of work to be in the top 1%. You have to be extremely vigilant of the current developments in your business and everything relevant to it. You must keep improving yourself on all aspects - be it communication, management, presentation skills, technical skills and anything you feel is relevant. Mentioned a few times earlier in this book, the skill of thinking ahead, anticipating how the customer will respond and being prepared for different direction of responses is how you control the conversation and in turn the project.

Staying ahead is keeping up to date. If you see a pattern here, yes, I'm saying it again. Keep learning as I've stated throughout this book. Businesses pay you to know what you're talking about and how your solutioning their investment. It doesn't pay well to sit back and relax once you have achieved a good position in the consultancy business. Keep improving as the business landscape keeps evolving and technology keeps changing.

Master Your Emotions, Stay Professional

Of course, you have to make your clients comfortable and make them trust you to go ahead with any advice. But all the interactions that you make should strictly reside within professional scope only. And remember to safeguard your own sanity when you work.

It is possible to get sucked in too much in a demanding career like that of a consultant and feel drained out emotionally. Avoid getting personal with your workplace and work. Remember at the end of the day, it is all just business and you are not saving the world. Take care of your physical and mental health.

Be Likeable

Being likeable is being genuine. That manager you feel you can always go to is how you want to be perceived by your peers and clients. I knew early on I had this skill set and I used it to my full advantage to move up in my career. I'm not saying always be smiling or looking at the positive side of problems, I'm saying be real. You're dealing with a wide spectrum of customers and they are putting their trust in you will only happen 100% when they feel they are dealing with a real person they can relate too. It's a real tightrope to walk here. Knowing when to reveal enough of yourself yet making sure it doesn't impact your performance as a specialist is what this skill requires. A good example is siding with the customer with a product or service limitation they really need and even bitching about it with them. Or, even getting personal enough to know your client's lives outside the business and revealing a bit about yourself. Do you both have children? Are you both dog lovers? These are some ways to connect at a different level. When times get rough, having that likability on your side will help smooth things out with the customer for time to time.

Chapter 8: Know When to Get Out

Ask yourself this important question tonight: *'Am I looking forward to work tomorrow?'* Take a little time for yourself and think about how happy you are with your career and work-life balance.

As mentioned earlier, being a master consultant is a huge responsibility and status that can be difficult to maintain. It takes a toll on your mind as well as your body. Your personal life and sanity need to be safeguarded at any cost because at the end of the day, that's all that matters. If your career demands you to suffer for the cause of it, you lose the entire point and your performances will not be up to standards.

When you take up a demanding career like that of a professional service consultant, it is important to know that there is a high possibility you will reach a boiling point. You must take time off to cool down. Working beyond such mental states and neglecting self-care will make you lose passion for the work that once you adored and found marvelous.

Remember it is okay to get out and take a break, whether temporary or permanent to rejuvenate yourself. Knowing when to get out is essential for a successful career and happy personal life.

Here are some key things to keep monitoring so you don't lose scope of the bigger picture, that is your happiness.

Physical Health

Physical health is the most important aspect of a fulfilling life. Your physical fitness can suffer when you keep ignoring the warning alarms your body makes. Are you too focused on your work that you are not taking care of yourself? It's probably time to take a step back and come up with a good fitness schedule and activities to keep your body healthy.

When you don't look after yourself well, it shows in your attitude. You will automatically lose the charm of a champion you need to be as a master consultant.

For each night you burn that midnight oil, you end up with a crappy day in the morning that will only lead to lowered productivity. Learn to manage your work timings effectively and fit in your fitness regimen to give you the maximum benefit.

A few minutes of physical activity a day like a brisk early morning walk, meditation and exercise can make a huge difference.

Taking care of your diet is another aspect of your physical health. Many consultants have the habit of skipping meals and following unhealthy food habits to cope with the traveling and busy work that they have to undertake. Don't fall into that abyss of choosing quick junk food to replace healthy regular meals. Always make time for a proper meal and make sure you stay energetic and look energetic.

Take care of your sleep patterns. Don't listen to pseudo-intellectuals bragging about the negligible duration of sleep that multi-billionaires have and assume it to be a mark of success. I for one think its bullshit. I know if I don't get a good night sleep, I'm not at my peak the following day. You have got to have a healthy amount of sleep to stay refreshed and feel confident with every business interaction you make. It's all about creating and following a routine.

Only a happy consultant can be a successful consultant.

Here are some ways to promote physical wellbeing in the workplace.

- Take time outs and go for breaks during lunch or tea times to de-stress.
- Choose friendly and pleasant environments to carry out your negotiations and talks where possible
- Take walks when you have been sedentary for a long period working at your desk.
- Remember to stretch your muscles to avoid back pain and neck pain associated with desk jobs. Download that app with reminders.
- Make use of ergonomically designed furniture if you have the luxury
- Schedule your breaks in your calendar so others see you're unavailable those times

At the least, allocate 30 minutes a day for physical activities. I assure you'll feel more energetic and engaging in your work.

Mental Health

Mental health often gets overlooked because most often, people feel that they simply don't have the time to worry about their worries. Stress is a real phenomenon and the more you choose to ignore, the nastier it gets. It is one of the worst feelings to experience and can completely ruin your days.

Stress is an invisible magical force that binds you. The effects of stress on your physical health are obvious. Ever felt increased heart rates? Migraines? How about restlessness? Or sleep deprivation?

As you grow your career as a consultant, your higher status may cause you to feel more stressed and consequently affect your peace of mind. When things get overwhelming - seek help, take a break, go on a vacation, do what makes you feel relaxed and peaceful. This will happen as you climb the corporate ladder, trying to prove yourself and facing new challenges. Prepare for it.

If your constantly faced with stressful situations, you need to de-stress and come out of it quickly. Failing to address stress can be like letting a slow poison enter your system. Take active measures like meditation, relaxing activities and even time off. Don't worry what others think. It's your journey, and your story. They are not part of it.

Your Drive

There is one important block that somehow trumps every other situation and makes you stagnant in your career. It is a lack of passion that you had during the start of your career. It's the one most important ingredient to continued growth and without passion, it becomes impossible to keep moving forward.

Lack of passion or a period of slump can happen to anyone in any profession. It's more so prevalent in careers like consulting. You would be doing it for so long that at a point you just lose the drive to do more. Everything seems repetitive and gets boring with all the experiences you have gathered. This has a huge impact on the quality of your work. Look for something new and exciting to get back the lost drive you once had. I know this has happened to me a few times throughout my journey. Especially when I've failed at something. You really should take a step away from it. I think it makes you strong knowing if that hungry comes back, then you're in the right career. Do not lose hope. It may take weeks or months to get back the passion you once had - which is exactly what happened to me.

Letting go and taking time off can be a rejuvenating process that you so badly need. As the saying goes "Fall down 7 times but stand up 8". Find the power to keep standing up whenever you fall no matter how long it takes.

Chapter 9: Outlook for Professional Service Consulting

Digital revolution is impacting the consulting industry, more than ever. This presents a tremendous set of opportunities for consultants to enhance the client experience.

Data analytics and AI is leading the show by identify and predict patterns, thus enabling you to service your clients better. It's likely that these technologies will keep adapting as there in the infancy stages. Our project methodologies have been unchanged for decades and won't change for a long time. However, Data analytics and AI will put and value-added service to our projects for example: pinpointing risk and letting us know exactly when it will happen. It will give us time to react and stay a step ahead which mentioned earlier is a key trait to be a master consultant.

Monitoring these technologies and staying up to date on your own time will open external opportunities for you. Although the initial learning curve could be a bit overwhelming, as you progress and make yourself fluent in the related technologies, the next adaptations will get easier to follow, and will help you sail smoothly. It's called momentum.

Being a professional service consultant is one of the most exciting and rewarding careers there is. But it comes with its own challenges and learning curve. As long as you have the drive and passion to go about it in the right way, you can achieve great heights and be a successful consultant and even start-up and run your own consulting firm successfully.

It does take hard work, smart work and a lot of experience to get to where you want to. Focus on building the right skills and welcoming mentorship from your contemporaries.

Remember it's hard to keep learning and sometimes frustrating. If you think you're good enough where you are, I'm fine with that. That's one less consultant I have to compete with ☺

Afterword

I truly appreciate you spending your time to read my book.
Visit masterconsultant.club for additional resources.

About the Author

Jason Bear is an accomplished professional services consultant with a decorative resume ranging from working for a number of small to mid-sized firms to one of the Big Four. He has led and played key roles in dozens of major transformation project along the way. By the age of 30, he opened his own Independent Consulting Company.